Thank Heavens for Dogs

To....

May God bless you with the
friendship of a loving dog.

From...

All things bright and beautiful,
all creatures great and small,
all things wise and wonderful,
the Lord God made them all.

Mrs Cecil Frances Alexander
Irish hymn-writer and poet, 1818–1895

God gave us dogs...
to teach us the meaning of unconditional love

A dog is the only thing on earth that will
love you more than you love yourself.

Josh Billings
American Humourist, 1818–1885

Not every person knows how to love a dog,
but every dog knows how to love a person.

1 John 4:7
Dear friends, let us love one another,
for love comes from God.
Everyone who loves has been born
of God and knows God.

(New International Version)

Happiness is a warm heart
and a wet nose

A hug is the shortest distance
between two friends

God gave us dogs...
to be our friends

Animals are such agreeable friends – they ask
no questions, they pass no criticisms.

George Eliot
English novelist, 1819–1880

Dogs are God's way of apologising
for outrageous relatives!

●

Dogs are fur-ever friends!

●

Whoever said diamonds are a girl's
best friend never owned a dog.

Anon

God gave us dogs...
to enrich our lives

Puppy dogs, fluffy dogs, big dogs,
small dogs, guard dogs, guide dogs,
rescue dogs, sniffer dogs, support dogs,
service dogs, lap dogs, loyal dogs,
hearing dogs, police dogs, pet dogs,
old dogs, soppy dogs, sheep dogs,
dogs of all shapes and sizes...

Thank you, God, for blessing us with
such a rich variety of dogs.

Psalm 107:1
O give thanks unto the LORD,
for he is good...
(King James Version)

God gave us dogs...
to make us smile

There's nothing like a puppy to
put a smile on your face,
joy in your soul and love in your heart.

●

If I had a pound for every time my dog made me
smile, I could give up work and retire tomorrow!

Anon

Whoever said you can't buy happiness
forgot little puppies.

Gene Hill
American writer and columnist, 1928–1997

Dogs laugh, but they laugh with their tails.

Max Eastman
American writer, 1883–1969

The eyes of a dog, the expression of a dog, the warmly wagging tail of a dog and the gloriously cold damp nose of a dog were, in my opinion, all God-given for one purpose only – to make complete fools of us human beings.

Barbara Woodhouse
British dog trainer and author of No Bad Dogs, *1910–1988*

God gave us dogs...
to demonstrate true love

The world would be a beautiful place if people had hearts that were as loving as a dog's heart.

Anon

Dogs, once they love, they love steadily, unchangingly, till their last breath.

Elizabeth von Arnim
British novelist, 1866–1941

Until one has loved an animal, a part of one's soul remains un-awakened.

Anatole France
French writer, 1844–1924

The only creatures that are evolved enough to convey pure love are dogs and infants.

Johnny Depp
American actor, 1963–present day

Dogs teach us loyalty

If having a soul means being able to feel
love and loyalty and gratitude then animals are
better off than humans.

•

The dog is the most faithful of animals
and would be much esteemed were
it not so common.
Our Lord God has made His greatest
gifts the commonest.

Martin Luther
*German theologian and key figure in the
Protestant Reformation, 1483–1546*

OK, I've posed
for the photo,
now throw
the tennis ball!

Dogs teach us forgiveness

I have a very old and very faithful
attachment for dogs.
I like them because they always forgive.

Albert Camus
French philosopher and author of The Fall, *1913–1960*

Think about a dog's ability to forgive.
This to me is love.

Cesar Millan
Mexican-American dog trainer and author of
How to Raise the Perfect Dog, *1969–present day*

To err is human, to forgive, canine.

Anon

Dogs show us how to forgive,
to let go of the past and to live
each day joyously.

Dogs are great role models

Dogs teach us that ...
It's fun to make new friends.
It's important to chase your dreams.
It's essential to make time for play.
It's great to learn new tricks.

'Let's humour the human
with a High Five!'

'Wake me up when the weekend arrives!'

Steve Harris: Abi takes a nap

Dogs show us how ...

To protect the people we love.
To sniff out new opportunities.
To explore the world with enthusiasm.
To take time for a much-needed snooze.

Can I have a snack
or a walk, and
preferably both?

Dogs make a difference

Every once in a while, a dog enters your life and changes everything for the better.

Dogs can lift your spirits when everyone else fails.

Dogs make life better

Dogs are not our whole life, but they
do make our lives whole.

Roger Caras
American author of A Celebration of Dogs, *1928–2001*

Once you have had a wonderful dog, a life
without one, is a life diminished.

Dean Koontz
American author of A Big Little Life: A Memoir of a Joyful Dog,
1945–present day

Psalm 103:5
He fills my life with good things...
(New Living Translation)

My dog does this amazing thing where
he just exists and makes my whole life better
because of it.

Anon

Dogs make great therapists

I have found that when you are deeply
troubled there are things you get from the silent
devoted companionship of a dog that you can
get from no other source.

Doris Day
American actress, 1922–present day

There is no better tonic than a warm bundle of
puppy with shining eyes, a waggy tale and
a licky tongue!

Anon

All the best therapists have fur and four legs and I'm the very best.

Dog owners live longer. Yes, really! A dog will capture your heart and also improve your heart health with all the increased fresh air and walking.

Anon

So, how about putting some snacks on this strange pink plate?

Dogs make splendid playmates

Dogs motivate us to play, be affectionate,
seek adventure and be loyal.

Tom Hayden
American author and politician, 1939–2016

We don't stop playing because we get old.
We get old because we stop playing.

Anon

Dogs make great personal trainers

A dog is one of the remaining reasons why some people can be persuaded to go for a walk.

Orlando Aloysius Battista
Canadian-American chemist and author,
1917–1995

An early-morning walk,
jog or run, with a dog
at your side, is a blessing
for the whole day.

Anon

Dogs help us to enjoy God's creation

Some of our greatest historical and artistic
treasures we place with curators in museums;
others, we take for walks.

Roger Caras
American author of A Celebration of Dogs, *1928–2001*

Life is simply better, richer, fuller,
healthier, happier, more satisfying,
more active and more fun with a dog!
And maybe a little messier and muddier, too!

Psalm 118:24
This is the day that the LORD
has made; let us rejoice and
be glad in it.
(New Revised Standard Version)

Blue skies, fresh air, wide open spaces – come on, humans, the world is waiting for us!

Dogs are great listeners

When I need someone to talk to,
someone to listen without interrupting,
someone to look at me with her head on one side
as if to say, '*I'm sorry you've had a tough day,
tell me all about it...*'
then my dog is the best listener in the world -
unless, of course, she smells a rabbit or spies a
tennis ball, then you might as well talk to the wind!

Anon

No one appreciates the very special genius of your
conversation as a dog does.

Christopher Morley
American author, 1890–1957

There are times when every human needs a listening ear, an outstretched paw and a loving heart.

Dogs always keep your secrets

A dog has lots of friends because he wags his tail
and not his tongue.

I can tell my dog anything,
knowing that he won't tell my children,
my wife or my mother-in-law.
Everyone needs a trustworthy friend like that!

Anon

Dogs are better than humans because
they know but do not tell.

Emily Dickinson
American poet, 1830–1886

I'm listening,
tell me more,
that's hilarious.

It's not what we have
in life that matters, but
who we have in our lives.

Dogs are great companions

When we are worried, there is
a sense of strength and encouragement
that we can get from the silent, devoted
companionship of a dog
that we can't get anywhere else.

Dogs have a way of finding the people
who need them and filling an emptiness
we didn't even know we had.

Anon

Dogs offer a warm welcome

A house is never lonely where a loving dog waits.

●

We can learn so much from dogs
about how to offer a warm welcome.
When I return home, my wife and children barely
bat an eyelid, but my dog greets me by jumping up
and down and wagging her tail in total ecstasy.
What's not to like?

Anon

Such short lives our pets have to spend with
us and they spend most of it waiting for us
to come home each day.

John Grogan
American writer, author of Marley and Me, *1957–present day*

So, what time do you call this?

Dogs make a house a home
(but it can always be repaired!)

For me a house or an apartment becomes
a home when you add one set of four legs,
a happy tail, and that indescribable measure
of love that we call a dog.

Roger Caras
American author of A Celebration of Dogs, *1928–2001*

When you arrive home ...
a dog makes you feel as if he has been waiting
to see you all day and now his day is complete!

•

Dogs leave paw prints on your heart
(and all over your floors, too!)

Anon

I've opened the post for you – nothing interesting, just bills!

These are not wrinkles,
they're my laugh lines!

Dogs accept you just the way you are...

A dog doesn't care how much you earn.
A dog doesn't care what car you drive.
A dog doesn't care if you're young or old.
A dog doesn't care if you're a bit overweight.
A dog doesn't care if your jokes are cringe-worthy.
A dog doesn't care about designer labels.
A dog just wants to love you
and spend time with you.

Caution... Don't accept your dog's admiration as conclusive evidence that you are wonderful.

Eppie Lederer
American advice columnist, 1918–2002

Destination Heaven

You think dogs will not be in heaven?
I tell you, they will be there before any of us.

Robert Louis Stevenson
Scottish writer, 1850–1894

God will prepare everything for our perfect
happiness in heaven, and if it takes my dog being
there, I believe he'll be there.

Billy Graham
American evangelist, 1918–present day

I heard someone describe heaven once, as a place
where, when you get there,
all the dogs you ever loved run to greet you.

Robert B. Parker
American crime writer, 1932–2010

Psalm 36:5-6

Your love is faithful, LORD...
Your decisions are always fair.
They are firm like mountains, deep
like the sea, and all people and
animals are under your care.

(Contemporary English Version)

Revelation 4:11

You are worthy, our Lord and God, to receive glory and honour and power, for you created all things, and by your will they were created and have their being.

(New International Version)